ULTIMATE UNOFFICIAL
SURVIVAL TACTICS
FOR
FORTNITE
BATTLE ROYALE
SHARPSHOOTER SECRETS FOR MASTERING YOUR ARSENAL

JASON R. RICH

Sky Pony Press
New York

Sky Pony Press books may be purchased in bulk at special discounts for sales promotion, corporate gifts, fund-raising, or educational purposes. Special editions can also be created to specifications. For details, contact the Special Sales Department, Sky Pony Press, 307 West 36th Street, 11th Floor, New York, NY 10018 or info@ skyhorsepublishing.com.

Sky Pony® is a registered trademark of Skyhorse Publishing, Inc.®, a Delaware corporation.

Visit our website at www.skyponypress.com.

10 9 8 7 6 5 4 3 2 1

Library of Congress Cataloging-in-Publication Data is available on file.

Cover design by Brian Peterson

Hardcover ISBN: 978-1-5107-4459-2
E-book ISBN: 978-1-5107-4467-7

Printed in China

TABLE OF CONTENTS

ULTIMATE UNOFFICIAL
SURVIVAL TACTICS
FOR
FORTNITE
BATTLE ROYALE

SHARPSHOOTER SECRETS FOR MASTERING YOUR ARSENAL

SECTION 1
WELCOME TO THE MYSTERIOUS ISLAND!

Each time you experience *Fortnite: Battle Royale*, you'll experience a high-intensity combat action/adventure game that requires you to control a single soldier who is placed on a mysterious island. Your soldier has just one purpose—to defeat and outlive up to 99 other soldiers during each match.

Fortnite: Battle Royale can be experienced—for free—on a PC, Mac, PlayStation 4, Xbox One, Nintendo Switch, Apple iPhone, Apple iPad, and on many Android-based smartphones and tablets.

Regardless of which gaming system you use, your experience playing this action-packed, combat-oriented game will be almost identical on each platform. Yet, because you're playing with up to 99 other gamers, each controlling their own soldiers in real time, each match you participate in will be different. The game will never get boring or repetitive, and it'll be extremely difficult to master.

After a ton of practice, even if you do become a top-ranked player and get really good at winning matches when participating in *Fortnite: Battle Royale*'s Solo game play mode (which is the most popular), you can always experience one of the other game play modes (such as Duos, Squads, Playground, or some type of 50 v 50 match), and have a totally different game play experience that's filled with new types of challenges.

No matter which game play mode you select, one thing you can be sure of is that during each match, the soldier you're controlling will need to participate in fast-paced and intense firefights and battles.

THE SIX SKILLS YOU'LL NEED TO MASTER
TO BECOME A SHARPSHOOTER

To consistently defeat your enemies in firefights and win #1 Victory Royale, you'll need to master the art of survival, be able to build quickly, avoid the deadly storm, and learn how to use the many guns and explosive weapons at your disposal. When it comes to working with weapons during a match, you'll consistently need to use six essential skills, including:

1. Finding weapons and then adding the best selection of them to your personal arsenal. The weapons you collect get stored within your soldier's backpack. It only has slots for up to five weapons and/or loot items (excluding your soldier's pickaxe, which can also be used as a short-range weapon).
2. Choosing the most appropriate weapon based on each combat situation. This means quickly analyzing the challenges and rivals you're currently facing, and selecting a close-range,

mid-range, or long-range gun, an explosive weapon, or a projectile explosive weapon that'll help you get the job done.

3. Collecting and stockpiling five different types of ammunition and making sure you have an ample supply of ammunition for each weapon you want to use.

4. Positioning yourself in the ideal location, with direct line-of-sight to your target(s), so you can inflict damage in the most accurate and efficient way possible. Headshots always cause more damage than a body shot, for example, when your targeting enemies.

5. Aiming each type of weapon so you're able to consistently hit your targets, without wasting ammunition or increasing the risk of your enemies having time to shoot back. When your soldier crouches down while shooting a weapon, their aim will always improve. Having to walk or run while shooting reduces your soldier's accuracy when aiming a weapon, but this is often necessary.

6. Shooting the active weapon your soldier is holding, and then quickly switching between weapons as needed.

Once you get good at performing each of these tasks, it'll still take a lot of practice to become a highly skilled sharpshooter who is capable of using single shots to defeat enemies. Plus, you'll need to discover how to best use the weapons at your disposal to destroy structures and fortresses in which your enemies may be hiding.

Learning how to effectively and efficiently use the many types of weapons at your disposal when playing **Fortnite: Battle Royale** is the main focus of this unofficial strategy guide.

GET ACQUAINTED WITH THE MYSTERIOUS ISLAND

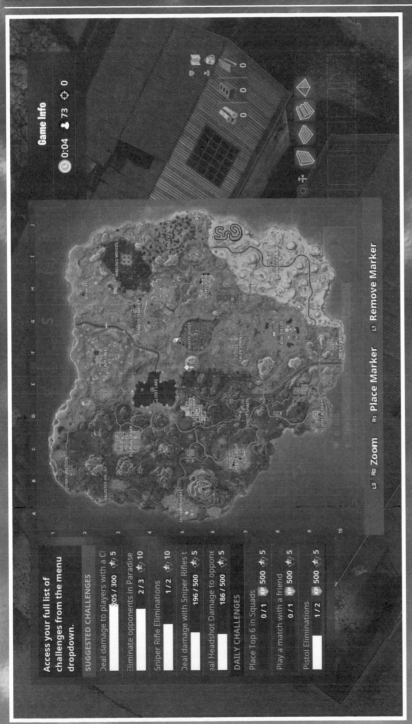

Each match you experience when playing *Fortnite: Battle Royale* takes place on a mysterious island. This island contains approximately twenty unique points of interest (locations) that are labeled on the island map. In addition, between these points of interest, you'll discover many smaller locations that also offer interesting or unique places to explore. (This is what the island looked like during the latter part of Season 5.)

Each location on the map offers a different type of terrain. As you explore, you'll encounter wide open and flat areas. In this situation, you'll want to run (not walk) in a zigzag pattern and keep jumping up and down to make yourself a fast-moving target that's difficult to hit.

Some terrain will feature hills, mountains, lakes, valleys, or desert areas, for example. Within many of these locations a few small structures (which are often worth searching) will often be scattered about.

Many areas contain single-family homes or smaller buildings.

Within a few areas, you'll encounter multi-story buildings positioned closely together. During your exploration, you'll also encounter farmhouses, stables, mining tunnels, mansions, factories, tall watch towers, storage container facilities, junk yards, grave yards, stone crypts, secret bases, camping lodges, and many other types of structures.

To survive during a match, it's important to always be mindful of your surroundings and discover unexpected and strategic ways to use the terrain around you to your tactical advantage.

Having a height advantage, so you're above your opponent and aiming your weapon(s) down at them, will almost always help you during a firefight.

Battles and firefights can take place anywhere on the island—outdoors, within any building or structure on the island, or in and around structures and fortresses that soldiers build themselves during matches.

Firefights can and will often take place with opposing soldiers having fortified themselves within structures or fortresses. In these situations, long-range weapons (like rifles with a scope) and projectile explosive weapons (like Rocket Launchers, Grenade Launchers, and Guided Missile Launchers) will be your most useful weapons.

Any object you encounter on the island can give you a tactical advantage or serve as shielding against an incoming attack. For example, your soldier can crouch down and hide behind solid objects, like a vehicle, building, or stone pile.

Have your soldier climb up onto building rooftops, or almost any other objects (like piles of cars), to give them a height advantage over their opponents.

Using four different-shaped building tiles, construct ramps, bridges, small structures, or massive fortresses. Building requires using the resources that your soldier collects and harvests while exploring the island.

There are four types of tiles that you can mix and match to build with. Each has a different shape. Shown here is a wall tile made from wood.

This is a floor/ceiling tile made from stone. Before building each tile, choose which material you'll build with. Your options include wood, stone, and metal. Wood is the fastest to build with, but is the weakest. It can ultimately be destroyed by enemy weapons or explosives with the least amount of effort. Stone takes longer to build with, but each tile can withstand a more powerful attack before being destroyed.

Shown here are three pyramid-shaped tiles. The one on the left is made of metal. The one in the middle is made of stone, and to the right is a pyramid tile made of wood. Metal is the strongest material to build with, but it takes the longest to construct. As each tile is being constructed, it's HP slowly increases until it's fully built. Each tile then has its own HP meter, which determines how much damage it can withstand before getting destroyed.

Here you can see **three ramp/stairs-shaped tiles**. When you build this tile shape from wood (left), a ramp is quickly constructed. When you build with stone (middle) or metal (right), stairs are automatically constructed. By facing a tile, you're able to see its HP meter. As you can see, the HP meter for the stone ramp is currently full (280 HP).

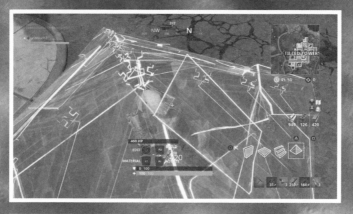

Pyramid-shaped tiles can be built on the roof of a structure or fortress and used as a ceiling. They can also be built around the roof of a fortress for your soldier to crouch behind as he or she peeks over the top to shoot at enemies. You're also able to build a pyramid-shaped tile directly over yourself, so it serves as a one-tile fortress. This one was constructed from metal.

Any structure you build can be edited to include a door or a window, or a hole in between levels, for example. A door makes it easier to enter or exit a structure, but also allows an enemy to easily follow you inside. One way to prevent this is to place Traps inside the structures and forts you build.

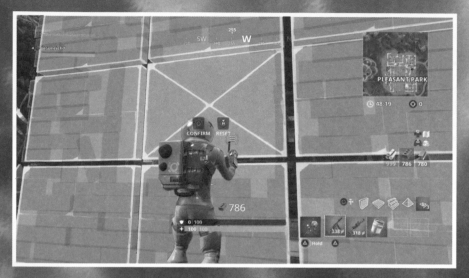

To create a window, face the tile where you want to build a window, enter Edit mode, and then select one or two of the squares. When you confirm your decision, the window gets built. The HP meter for the tile will change, often making it weaker.

Building windows into your fortress allows you to see out, plus shoot at your enemies, but it also allows them to see in and shoot at you. An enemy can easily toss a Grenade or shoot a Rocket Launcher, Grenade Launcher, or Guided Missile Launcher through a structure's window and know it'll inflict damage and potentially defeat anyone inside.

When building a fortress, you're typically better off building pyramid-shaped tiles around the outer edge, and then peeking out and hiding behind the tiles when you're ready to shoot at enemies. This offers greater protection. However, your enemies will likely be watching for your soldier's head to peek out, and that's when they'll start shooting. If they have a rifle with a scope and good aim, you could become the victim of a headshot.

Knowing what to build, which material to build with, where to build, and how to use what you build to your offensive or defensive advantage, are all decisions that will go hand-in-hand with your combat skills during a match.

WAYS TO GET AROUND THE ISLAND

The mysterious island is rather massive. There are several ways you can get around. For example, your soldier can walk, run, jump, or tiptoe.

One of the fastest ways to get around the island is to find and drive (or ride in) an All Terrain Kart (ATK). These souped-up golf carts can typically be found within Lazy Links and Paradise Palms (as well as the unlabeled points of interest around Paradise Palms, including the Racetrack). Once you find one, an ATK can be driven almost anywhere, across any type of terrain.

It's also possible to use Shopping Carts, Launch Pads, Bouncer Pads, Rifts (if available), a Rift-to-Go item (if available), and/or Jetpacks (if available) to get around the island faster.

A Bouncer Pad can be placed on any flat surface, as well as at a diagonal on a ramp. When your soldier steps on it, he'll be catapulted up into the air. Use the navigational controls to travel horizontally across a decent distance as your soldier is falling back to the ground. He won't be injured by the fall. To travel even farther, use a Launch Pad or Rift-to-Go item instead.

Shopping Carts can be found randomly around the island. You can push and then ride them. These can help you travel a good distance quickly if you start off on the top of a hill or mountain and ride downward.

Regardless of where you go on the island, you're eventually going to encounter enemies and be forced to engage in battle. Depending on the strategy you adopt early on, you might be able to avoid enemy contact during the early portions of a match while you're building up your arsenal, collecting resources, and gathering ammunition. As you get closer to the End Game, you'll find enemy soldiers, or they'll find you, and battles will ensue.

However, if you start off a match by landing in a popular point of interest, you're virtually guaranteed to encounter enemies and be forced into battle within moments.

Always be prepared to encounter enemies wherever you go, especially when you're inside a building or structure. Enemies can also hide outside and wait to launch an ambush as you approach. Keep in mind, your enemies may booby trap a structure or object (such as a Loot Llama or ATK) that you might enter into or choose to approach. (Or you can set booby traps for your enemies.) Based on the type of terrain you're in, have an appropriate weapon in hand, and then be ready to defend yourself or aggressively attack the enemies you encounter.

TIPS FOR RAMP BUILDING

To reach otherwise inaccessible areas both inside structures and anywhere outdoors, you'll often need to build ramps and bridges. As you'll discover, there are different types of ramps you can build, based on your objective and the level of protection you need against incoming attacks.

When inside a building, to reach its attic, go to the highest floor and then build a ramp up to the ceiling. Use your soldier's pickaxe to smash through the ceiling to enter an attic. Within many single-family homes on the island, it's within the attic (or basement) where you'll often discover chests.

In this stable, to reach the chest that's often found up in the loft area, it's necessary to build a ramp.

Build an over-under ramp to help you reach an area that's higher up, while simultaneously protecting yourself from enemies that may shoot at you from above. Building this type of ramp takes twice the amount of resources of a regular ramp, but the added protection is often well worth it.

When you build a double ramp (two ramps side-by-side), your soldier can zigzag in between the two ramps as they climb upward, so an enemy who is below can't determine your soldier's exact location. If one ramp is about to be destroyed by an enemy, your soldier can leap to the other ramp and buy themselves a few extra seconds of safety.

To increase a ramp's structural integrity and make it more difficult to destroy, be creative and utilize more complex ramp designs like these. Consider building them out of stone or metal, so they can withstand the most damage.

One of the biggest drawbacks to quickly building tall ramps made out of wood is that an enemy soldier can easily shoot and destroy just one tile near the bottom of a ramp, and the whole thing will come crashing down with your soldier still on it. Your soldier can withstand a fall from up to three levels and receive little or no damage, but a fall from a greater height will cause damage or even defeat.

KEEP YOUR SOLDIER'S HEALTH AND SHIELD METERS MAXED OUT

A firefight typically involves you shooting a gun at one or more of your enemies, and at the same time, they'll be shooting back at you. The player with the best aim, the most powerful weapon, and the quickest reflexes will typically win a firefight.

Every soldier has both a Health and Shield meter. At the start of a match, the Health meter (which is displayed as a green bar near the bottom-center of the screen on most gaming systems) is maxed out at 100 HP.

The Shield meter (a blue bar that's displayed directly above the Health meter) starts off at 0 HP but can be activated and replenished using a variety of loot item powerups, like Shield Potions. Shown here, the soldier's Shield meter is at 50 out of 100. This can be boosted by drinking the Small Shield Potion he's carrying in the right-most backpack slot.

Each time your soldier gets injured during a firefight (that involves guns or explosives), first some of their Shield meter (if its active) gets depleted with each hit, and then their Health meter begins to diminish. Shields can help keep a soldier alive longer by protecting them from incoming bullets or explosions, but shields do not protect against damage from the storm or injury resulting from a fall.

As soon as a soldier's Health meter reaches zero, they're defeated and immediately eliminated from the match.

To replenish Health HP during a match, a variety of powerup loot items, including Apples, Bandages (shown here), Cozy Campfires, Med Kits, Slurp Juice, and Chug Jugs are available. These items (with the exception of Apples) can be found, grabbed, stored within a soldier's backpack, and then used or consumed when they're needed to prolong a soldier's survival. Each one takes a different amount of time to consumer or use, during which time, your soldier cannot move, build, or use a weapon (so he or she is vulnerable to attack).

Ideally, before entering into a firefight or battle, you want your soldier's Health and Shield meters to be maxed out at 100.

If you're playing *Fortnite: Battle Royale*'s Duos or Squads game play mode, this means you'll be working with either one partner or a team of up to three other soldiers (your squad) during a match. As long as each of the players are using a gaming headset with a built-in microphone, everyone can speak with each other throughout the match to coordinate attacks and plan strategies.

During a Duos, Squads, or 50 v 50 match, anytime a soldier gets injured, that soldier will not be able to do anything but crawl around helplessly as their Health meter slowly decreases. In this situation, try to crawl to a safe area.

While a soldier is injured, a partner or squad member (or a team member if you're playing a 50 v 50 match) can revive an injured soldier and bring them back to health. This must be done before the injured soldier's Health meter hits zero. Soldiers who revive their partner, squad mates, or team members are rewarded, just as they're rewarded for defeating enemies during battles.

BEWARE OF THE DEADLY STORM

Within moments after your soldier (along with up to 99 other soldiers) step foot on the island, a deadly storm materializes and then steadily grows and moves across the island. At the start of a match, the entire island is inhabitable and safe to explore.

As the storm moves and expands, more and more of the island becomes uninhabitable. These areas are displayed in pink on the island map.

A soldier can survive for a short time within a storm-ravaged area, but for every second they're caught in the storm, some of their Health meter gets depleted. The negative impact of the storm on a soldier's Health meter intensifies during the later stages of a match.

It's not possible to outrun the storm for a long time. If a soldier gets caught in the storm for too long, he or she will perish. It's important to pay careful attention to the storm's path, so you can avoid it. When you look at the Location Map (the small map that's continuously displayed on the screen) your soldier's exact location is depicted using a white triangle icon. If a white line also appears, this is the route to follow to avoid the storm or get out of it the fastest. The timer displayed immediately below the Location Map tells you when the storm will move and expand next.

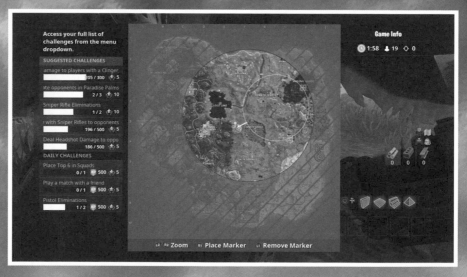

By looking at the island map, you can easily determine the areas of the island that are already uninhabitable. These areas are displayed in pink. The larger circle on the map shows the current safe area of the island that has not yet been ravaged by the storm. When an inner circle is displayed on the island map, this shows you where the safe area will be once the storm moves and expands again. You always want to be in in the safe area before the storm arrives.

As the storm moves and expands, this pushes all the soldiers who remain alive on the island into a smaller and smaller area, until the End Game, when only a small area of the island is still inhabitable, and the few remaining soldiers are forced to fight. Each match lasts about fifteen minutes when playing the Solo, Duos, or Squads game play mode.

The last few minutes of each match are referred to as the End Game or Final Circle, because only a small handful of soldiers remain alive, and the area where the final battles take place is very small. Remember, only one soldier (when playing Solo mode) will leave the island alive. Everyone else must be defeated or perish.

UNDERSTAND HOW TO READ THE ISLAND MAP

Whenever you switch to the island map view, you'll discover it's divided into quadrants. Along the top of the map are the letters "A" through "J." Along the left edge of the map are the numbers "1" through "10." Each point of interest (location) on the map can be found by its unique coordinates.

For example, Tilted Towers is found at map coordinates D5.5, and Snobby Shores is located at coordinates A5. At the start of Season 5, Paradise Palms replaced Moisty Mire and was centered around map coordinates L8, while Anarchy Acres was replaced by Lazy Links at map coordinates F2.5. The unlabeled Viking village (which contains the Viking ship) can be found on a mountaintop near map coordinates B4.5.

The drive-in movie theater (known as Risky Reels) is located at map coordinates H2. This location was fully renovated during the latter part of Season 5. Of course, you'll also discover chests, as well as weapons, ammo, loot items, and resource icons in and around the parked cars, as well as in the buildings surrounding the theater area.

If you're the first to reach the large shed containing picnic tables (located near the playground), you'll often find one or two chests, along with other items lying on the ground. A visit to Risky Reels is one of many locations where you can quickly build or expand your soldier's arsenal.

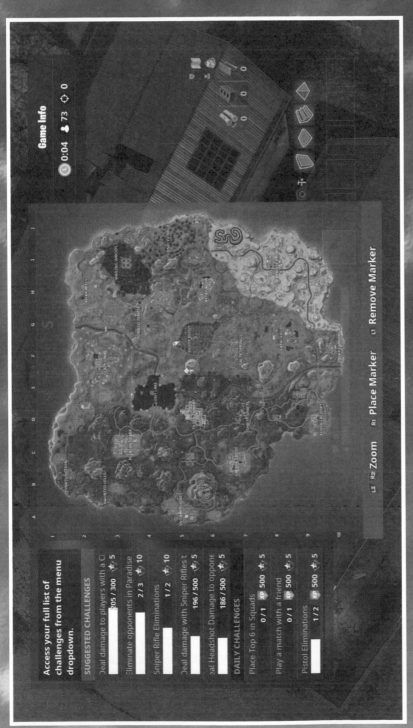

The island is comprised of about twenty points of interest that are labeled on the island map. This is what the island map looked like during Season 5. There are also a growing number of locations that are not labeled on the map, but that are well worth exploring.

Here's what you can see on the island map during a match:

- The random route the Battle Buses will take across the island. This route is only displayed while you're in the pre-deployment area and for the first few seconds while aboard the Battle Bus. Look for the blue line made up of arrow icons.
- The location of each point of interest on the island. The major points of interest are labeled. Many of the smaller points of interest, located between the major points of interest, are not labeled.
- Your current location. This is displayed as a white triangle icon.
- The location of your partner, squad mates, or team members, depending on which game play mode you're experiencing. Each player is displayed as a colored triangle.
- The current location of the storm. The storm-ravaged areas are always displayed in pink.
- The area of the island that's currently inhabitable is displayed inside the large circle on the map.
- Where the safe area (inhabitable land) on the island will be after the storm moves and expands next is displayed within the inner circle you'll often see on the island map.
- If markers have been placed on the map, these too are displayed. Markers are used to select a rendezvous location or desired landing location. Markers are placed by gamers on the island map for only you and your allies (not your enemies) to see.

Once you set markers on the island map, colored flares (one representing each marker) appear on the main game screen. Use a marker/flare to set a meetup location anytime during a match.

Check the timer (displayed directly below the Location Map) frequently to determine when the storm will be expanding and moving next, and make sure you're able to avoid the storm as much as possible.

Remember, the storm moves faster than your soldier can run, so unless you have an All Terrain Kart, Shopping Cart, Bouncer Pads, Launch Pads, Jetpack, plan to find and use Rifts, or have acquired a Rift-to-Go item, don't plan on trying to outrun the storm if you'll need to cover a long distance.

ALWAYS BE PREPARED FOR SOMETHING NEW

Every week or two, Epic Games releases a game update (also called a "patch"). In conjunction with each update, expect any of the following changes:

- New weapons or loot items are introduced into the game.
- The power and/or capability of specific weapons and/or loot items is tweaked.
- New (unlabeled) areas are added to the map (located between the labeled points of interest).
- One or more temporary game play modes are introduced.
- Specific loot items, weapons, or other game elements are "vaulted," meaning that they're removed from the game, but could be re-introduced at any time in the future.
- New outfits and items are added to the Item Shop.
- New Free Challenges and Battle Pass challenges are introduced.

Anytime something new is added, or changes are made to the game, a News screen is displayed when you launch the game. You can also visit: www.epicgames.com/fortnite /en-US/news for more information.

In addition to the regular game updates, every two to three months, Epic Games introduces a new gaming season. This is when major changes are made to the island map, and other significant alterations are made to various game play elements.

Also, in conjunction with each new season, a new Battle Pass is made available for purchase, and a new series of Battle Pass challenges are introduced. Acquiring a Battle Pass costs money. To learn more about them, visit: www.epicgames.com/fortnite/en-US/battle-pass.

This unofficial strategy guide was created during Season 5. If you're playing *Fortnite: Battle Royale* during Season 6 or beyond, expect the island map to be different, and for a variety of new loot items and weapons to be available to you.

SECTION 2

PREPARING FOR *FORTNITE: BATTLE ROYALE* MATCHES

Each time you launch *Fortnite: Battle Royale*, you'll find yourself in the Lobby.

From here, access the Settings menus to customize your game play experience. To do this, access the main game menu, and select the gear-shaped Settings icon. From the Game submenu, scroll through the icons near the top-center of the screen to access each of the submenus. Each submenu offers a selection of options you can tweak.

It's also from the Lobby that you can access the Battle Pass screen to purchase a Battle Pass, or purchase and unlock individual Battle Pass tiers to receive the prizes associated with each tier without completing the necessary challenges. It's also possible to review the challenges and prizes associated with each of the tiers for the current Battle Pass.

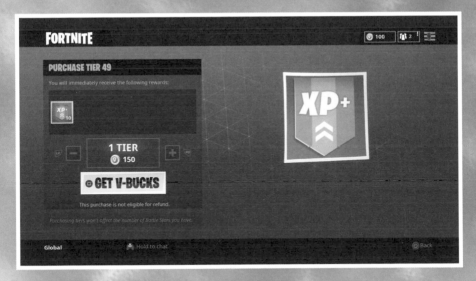

If you don't feel like completing individual tier-based challenges after purchasing a Battle Pass for the current game season, unlock one tier at a time with a 150 V-Buck purchase.

Access the Challenges screen to review the free challenges that anyone can complete while playing *Fortnite: Battle Royale* in order to unlock prizes. Whether or not you attempt to complete these challenges is optional.

TYPES OF OPTIONAL IN-GAME PURCHASES *FORTNITE: BATTLE ROYALE* OFFERS

Visit the Store to purchase bundles of V-Bucks. This is in-game currency used to purchase a Battle Pass, unlock Battle Pass tiers, or to purchase items (such as outfits) from the Item Shop. The more V-Bucks you purchase at once, the bigger discount you receive. Making purchases while playing *Fortnite: Battle Royale* is always optional.

Everyday, a different section of items, including outfits, pickaxe designs, glider designs, and emotes, are available from the Item Shop. It's here you can purchase items that allow you to alter the appearance of your soldier. Regardless of how you change your soldier's appearance, this is for cosmetic purposes only and it does not give your soldier any tactical advantage whatsoever.

Each time you select and purchase an item (such as this Ventura outfit with matching back bling) from the Item Shop, it gets stored within the Locker. It becomes yours to keep forever. Battle Passes expire at the end of each gaming season. Items purchased from the Item Shop (or that you unlock) never expire.

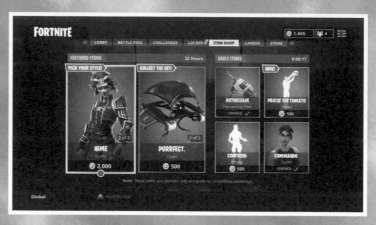

When visiting the Item Shop, the Featured Items displayed on the left tend to be "Legendary," meaning they're limited edition and only available for a short time. They also tend to be the most expensive. Some (but not all) outfits that cost 2,000 V-Bucks (about $20.00 US) come with a matching back bling (backpack) design, which is considered a separate item when it's stored within the Locker.

The Daily Items displayed on the right side of the screen within the Item Shop tend to be more common and less expensive. These become available for 24 to 48 hours but will be re-introduced in the Item Shop every few weeks or months. It's also within the Daily Items section where you'll find emotes (mostly dance moves) sold.

WHAT YOU SHOULD KNOW ABOUT EMOTES

There are three types of emotes offered in *Fortnite: Battle Royale*. These are used to showcase emotion or personality to other players while in the pre-deployment area or during a match. Some players use emotes as a greeting. Others use them to gloat after defeating an enemy. The three types of emotes include dance moves (shown here), spray paint tags, and graphic icons.

It's possible to purchase or unlock one dance move at a time. You can then perform two or three different dance moves back-to-back during a match to show off some lit choreography. Epic Games has created and released many different dance moves, each of which are available separately.

Graphic icon emotes get tossed into the air and are displayed for a few seconds before disappearing. Everyone nearby will see it when it's displayed. Most graphic emotes need to be unlocked by completing challenges or are given away as part of a Twitch Prime Pack, for example. To learn more about Twitch Prime Packs, visit: https://help.twitch.tv/customer/en/portal/articles/2572060-twitch-prime-guide.

Every soldier carries with them virtual spray paint and can tag any flat surface on the island once one or more spray paint tags are acquired. These are usually offered as prizes for completing challenges and are not sold within the Item Shop.

After acquiring a few different spray paint tags, mix and match them while you're on the island to create some eye-catching graffiti.

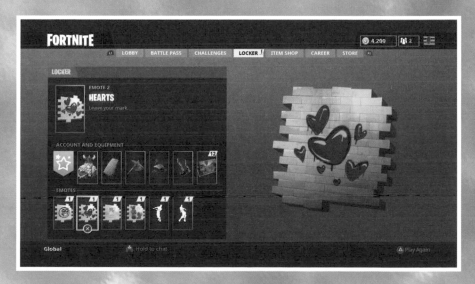

During each match, a soldier can carry up to six different emotes. Before a match, access the Locker and from below the Emotes heading, decide how you'll fill up the six emotes slots using any combination of emotes you've unlocked, purchased, or acquired.

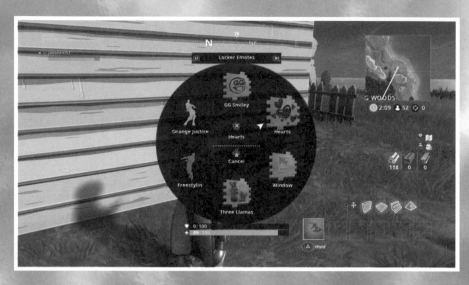

Anytime you're on the island (in the pre-deployment area or during a match), to use an emote, access this Emotes Menu and select which emote you want to showcase or use.

CHOOSE YOUR SOLDIER'S OUTFIT AND RELATED CUSTOMIZATION ITEMS

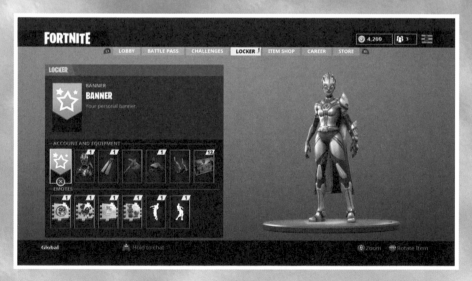

The tools for customizing the appearance of a soldier have become very popular. Once you purchase, unlock, or acquire one or more outfits and related items, before a match, visit the Locker. From under the Account and Equipment heading, one at a time, choose an outfit, back bling (backpack) design, pickaxe design, glider design, and contrail design that you want to use during the upcoming match. Once you select options from the Locker, they remain active in all future matches until you return to the Locker and alter them.

For each outfit that Epic Games releases, a matching back bling design, pickaxe design, and glider design are typically offered (and often sold separately). However, once you've acquired several different designs, you can mix and match them to create a unique look for your soldier. Shown here, the Magnus outfit, cape (back bling), pickaxe design, and glider are all part of the Norse set that has a Viking theme. This outfit set was introduced at the same time the Viking village (found near map coordinates B6) was introduced into the game during Season 5.

Some outfits (like Oblivion, Omen, and Raven), with their related items, will make your soldier look mean, tough, mysterious, or scary.

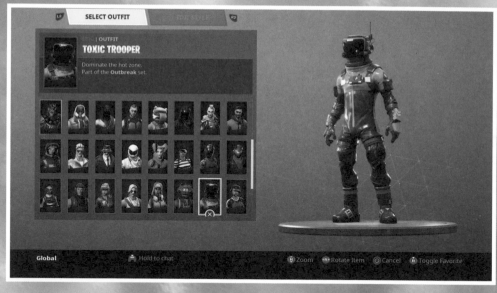

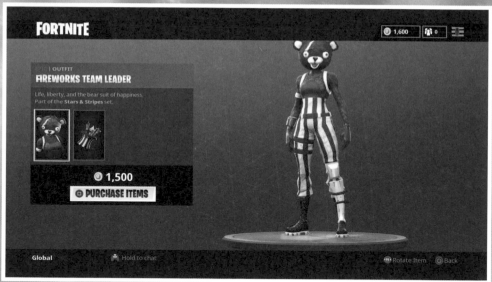

Some outfits (like Toxic Trooper) are tied into a theme or storyline introduced into the game, while some have something to do with a holiday (like Fireworks Team Leader for the July 4th holiday) or a special event happening in the real world.

An ever-growing selection of optional outfits, such as Tomatohead, Mullet Marauder, Leviathan, and Chomp Sr. are whimsical, light-hearted, and sometimes downright ridiculous.

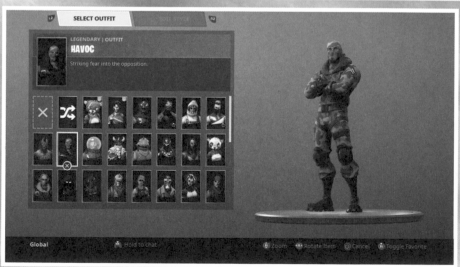

Of course, there are a wide range of outfits (including Carbide, Rose Team Leader, Warpaint, and Havoc), along with related items, that make your soldier look like a well-trained member of the military who's prepared to engage in combat. How you make your soldier look during a match is entirely up to you.

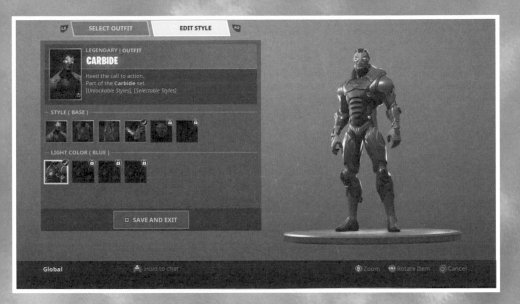

A growing number of the newer outfits allow you to use the Edit Style option to further customize the appearance of an outfit by unlocking and choosing different style-related features. When this option is available from the Locker, the Edit Style button will light up (near the top-right corner of the screen) when previewing an outfit.

To unlock the additional styles that are available for certain outfits, sometimes it's necessary to complete a series of challenges. On the right, the "Tomatohead Challenges" are described. These were available for a limited time during Season 5. Upon completing the challenges, the Tomatohead crown (shown on the right) was unlocked, but only if you also already owned the Tomatohead outfit.

Since the main focus of this unofficial strategy guide is on using weapons to defeat enemies, one thing to consider when choosing an outfit is how it will look during battle. If you choose a bright-colored, oversized outfit, such as Cuddle Team Leader or Rabbit Raider, you will stand out and be easier to spot and target by your enemies. If you choose an outfit that's bright pink, for example, you will get noticed!

SELECT A GAME PLAY MODE AND GET READY FOR ACTION!

When you're ready to participate in a match, from the Lobby, access the Choose Game Mode menu and select a game play mode. If you've selected Duos, Squads, or a game play mode that requires you to work with one or more other gamers, from directly above the Accept option, choose between the Fill and Don't Fill option. By choosing the Fill option, the game will automatically match you up with random gamers. Choose the Don't Fill option if you want to play with your online friends.

After returning to the Lobby, select the Play option to enter a match.

All gamers are immediately transported to the pre-deployment area. You'll wait here until up to 99 other gamers join the match. Feel free to explore, interact with other soldiers, test out weapons, or practice building. You cannot be injured or defeated in the pre-deployment area. Anything you collect, however, will be left behind once you board the Battle Bus.

During your stay in the pre-deployment area or for the first few seconds you're aboard the Battle Bus, access the island map to see the random route the Battle Bus will follow over the island. This information can help you choose the ideal landing location.

Once you're aboard the Battle Bus, enjoy the ride. Choose the exact moment you want to leap from the bus and free fall toward the island to reach your desired landing spot.

During your soldier's free fall, use the directional controls to navigate. To increase your soldier's falling speed, point him or her downward.

To slow down your soldier's rate of descent, and to avoid landing on the island with a fatal splat, activate their glider. (If you wait too long to manually activate the glider, it will automatically deploy for you to ensure a safe landing.) Once the glider is deployed, you'll have much more precise navigational control over your soldier's landing.

As soon as your soldier steps foot on the island, immediately look for and grab at least one weapon and some ammo. Otherwise, the only tool at your soldier's disposal is their pickaxe, which can be used as a close-range weapon, but it's weak. You'll need to hit an opponent multiple times with the pickaxe to cause any significant damage or defeat an enemy.

Many (but not all) chests remain in the same place from match to match, so once you discover their locations, remember them. That way you can return to each chest location during future matches and collect what's inside. During each match, each chest can only be opened once, so you want your soldier to be the first to find them.

CHOOSE THE IDEAL LANDING LOCATION

While you're aboard the Battle Bus, you'll need to choose a desired landing location. This decision can be made, in part, based on the random route the Battle Bus will take across the island.

During the time your soldier is free falling (or using their glider), you can navigate, and often soar through the air across at least half the length of the island. For example, if your intended destination is Lucky Landing (at map coordinates F10), but the route the Battle Bus will take doesn't go directly over this point of interest, chances are you can still reach that area by jumping off the bus at a point that comes closest to Lucky Landing, and then navigate your soldier while he or she is airborne.

There are a few different strategies gamers often use when choosing their landing locations. Here are some suggestions.

LAND DIRECTLY WITHIN A POPULAR POINT OF INTEREST

You can land in the heart of a popular point of interest, and plan to engage enemies in battle within moments after landing. This strategy works best for skilled gamers, who are already familiar with the area. They know exactly where to find and grab a weapon (and ammo) immediately.

LAND IN THE OUTSKIRTS OF A POPULAR POINT OF INTEREST

When you avoid landing directly within a popular point of interest, you're much less likely to encounter enemies right away. This allows you to spend a few minutes building up your arsenal and gathering resources, before entering the populated area where enemies are likely lurking about.

Since you'll be well armed and will have had a chance to activate your soldier's shields, you'll be able to more easily defeat the enemies you eventually encounter, or at least defend yourself against attacks. The drawback is that many of the chests and other weapons, ammo, and loot items that could have been found in the area will already have been picked clean.

By waiting a few minutes before entering a popular point of interest, you'll allow time for the other soldiers who did land there to fight amongst themselves. When you eventually enter the area, there will be fewer soldiers remaining. Plus, some that did survive will move on to other locations.

Keep in mind, anytime you, a partner, a squad mate, or a team member defeats an enemy during a match, the defeated soldier drops all of the weapons, ammo, loot items, and resources he or she was carrying. You're then able to grab whatever you want from the ground. This is an excellent way to build up your arsenal and gather resources you'll likely need. Shown here is the tail end of an epic firefight that involved a bunch of soldiers during a 50 v 50 match. Multiple soldiers were eliminated and wounded within a few moments.

This hut is located on a mountain just outside of Tilted Towers. Land on top of this hut. If you discover a chest (in the loft area), open it and grab what's inside. Also grab any weapons, ammo, and loot items you find out in the open within this hut. Once you're nicely armed, chop down a few nearby trees to gather some resources, and then slide down the cliff and enter Tilted Tower to face whatever challenges await. You'll find huts, houses, buildings, or structures that contain useful weapons, ammo, and loot items immediately outside almost every point of interest on the island.

LAND IN A REMOTE AND UNPOPULAR AREA

There are many remote areas of the island where few if any soldiers bother to land. By choosing one of these as your landing location, you'll have plenty of time to explore the area, build up your arsenal, gather resources, and collect loot items—without encountering any enemies.

Meanwhile, while you're building up your arsenal and preparing for the End Game without being bothered, your enemies who landed in the popular points of interest will be engaged in firefights. Some will survive, but many will not.

This strategy offers fewer opportunities to defeat enemies during the early stages of a match, but it greatly improves your chances of survival, and provides a better opportunity to gather a powerful arsenal that'll be useful during the End Game.

The house with a wooden tower on top of it that's found outside of Wailing Woods (between map coordinates I3 and J3) is a perfect example of a remote location where you should consider landing. Within the house and tower, you'll find at least two or three chests, plus a bunch of weapons, ammo, loot items, and resources lying out on the ground. Within the house's garage, there's sometimes an All Terrain Kart you can use to quickly drive to your next destination.

Another example of a remote landing location is the massive wooden tower located outside of Lonely Lodge (near map coordinates J5.5). By landing on top of the tower and working your way down, you'll often discover multiple chests, as well as other useful weapons, ammo, and loot items on the stairs.

POPULAR POINTS OF INTEREST CHANGE

Anytime Epic Games introduces a new labeled or unlabeled point of interest on the island, it immediately becomes popular. Thus, you can expect to encounter a bunch of enemy soldiers right away if you choose to land within one of these locations.

Based on the random route the Battle Bus follows, many gamers tend to leap from the bus either right at the start of the journey, or at the very last possible moment. As a result, any point of interest that's close to the beginning or end of the route will be popular during that match. In this case, Lazy Links and Risky Reels are at the start of the route, and Flush Factory and Lucky Landing are near the end.

Because Dusty Divot and what remains of Loot Lake are located near the center of the island, the Battle Bus almost always passes directly over one or both of these locations. Expect to encounter a bunch of enemy soldiers at either or both of these locations if you choose to land at one of them. In future gaming seasons, Dusty Divot or Loot Lake may be replaced by new points of interest, so this applies to any location located near the center of the island.

SECTION 3

OVERVIEW OF WEAPONS AND HOW TO USE THEM

To excel when playing *Fortnite: Battle Royale*, you need to become skilled at shooting and using all the different types of weapons available to your soldier during a match.

It's important to understand that new weapons are introduced regularly, while other weapons get vaulted (removed from the game), or nerfed (meaning their capabilities are tweaked and sometimes made less powerful).

No matter how much you know about each weapon (in terms of facts and statistics about it), nothing replaces the need to practice using them over and over again within the game, in as many different combat scenarios as possible.

The top-ranked *Fortnite: Battle Royale* gamers have all practiced aiming and shooting with each weapon to the extent that they've developed their *muscle memory*, which means they no longer need to think too much about which weapon to select for a particular task, and then spend valuable seconds considering the best approach for aiming and firing that weapon during each firefight or battle.

WHAT IS MUSCLE MEMORY?

The concept of establishing and using your muscle memory applies when playing almost any computer or video game. The goal is to practice playing, and repeat the same actions so often, that they become second nature to you. In other words, you train yourself to know exactly what to press on the keyboard and/or mouse, and know exactly when to do it, so you don't need to waste time thinking about it. Muscle memory can only be developed through repetition and practice . . . lots and lots of practice.

In terms of playing **Fortnite: Battle Royale**, with practice, you'll want to train your muscle memory to help you accomplish common tasks, including:

- Quickly switching between and selecting weapons within your backpack.
- Aiming your selected weapon and firing accurately at your targets.
- Switching between building, resource collection/harvesting, and fighting mode.
- Quickly building structures and being able to switch between building tile shapes and building materials.
- Accessing the island map, Emotes menu, and Quick Chat menu during a match.

HOW AND WHERE TO FIND AND COLLECT WEAPONS

Your soldier's arsenal always includes a pickaxe. This item cannot be dropped. The primary use of a pickaxe is to harvest wood, stone, and metal—the three core resources used for building (and to acquire items from Vending Machines). However, the pickaxe can also be used as a close-range weapon.

Each time you land on the island after leaping from the Battle Bus, your soldier's only weapon is their pickaxe. It's not very powerful, however, and it's no match against an enemy who's holding a gun or explosive weapon. In fact, you'll need to hit your enemy multiple times with the pickaxe to defeat him.

At any given time, your soldier can also hold up to five additional weapons and/or loot items within their backpack's slots. It's your responsibility to find and grab the best selection of weapons and loot items, based on the challenges you anticipate facing.

For example, if you're about to search a group of single-family homes, when you encounter enemies within those homes, you'll need to engage in close-range firefights. Knowing this, you'll want to have at least one type of Pistol or Shotgun within your arsenal (along with an ample supply of compatible ammunition).

There are multiple ways to find and collect weapons on the island, including:

Grab weapons that you find lying on the ground, out in the open.

Weapons can also be found within chests.

You'll typically find more powerful weapons (based on Rarity) within Supply Drops and Loot Llamas. Anytime you approach a Supply Drop or Loot Llama, proceed with extreme caution. Enemies often stake these out, wait for an enemy to approach, and then launch a surprise attack.

In this case, the Supply Drop landed on the side of a cliff. When opened, its contents will slide down the cliff, so it will take longer to retrieve them. To quickly fix this situation, build a floor tile under the Supply Drop, so it'll catch its contents when you open it.

If an enemy has a sniper rifle with a scope, they can position themselves far away from the Supply Drop or Loot Llama and still shoot at enemies with extreme accuracy.

It's also possible to booby trap a Loot Llama using Remote Explosives. Once these explosives are placed near the Loot Llama (in this case directly in front of and behind it), the soldier setting the Trap can hide nearby and then detonate these explosives when an enemy gets close.

As soon as you approach a Loot Llama or Supply Drop that's out in the open, quickly build walls around it to protect yourself and the Loot Llama's contents. Metal walls were built here to provide maximum protection. Don't forget to add a roof on top of the structure to prevent (or slow down) attacks from above.

Another way to expand your arsenal, and often obtain more powerful weapons, is to defeat enemies and collect what they leave behind as they're eliminated from the match.

Weapons can also be acquired from Vending Machines that are randomly placed throughout the island. Trade your collected (or harvested) resources for individual items being offered by a Vending Machine. Each Vending Machine offers a different selection of weapons and loot items.

When playing a Duos, Squads, or 50 v 50 match, for example, you can also trade weapons, loot items, ammo, and resources with your partner, squad mates, or team members. To do this, access your soldier's Backpack Inventory screen, highlight the weapon you want to share, and then use the Drop command. The weapon will drop to the ground and a nearby soldier can pick it up.

Anytime your backpack is full and you come across another weapon (or loot item) you want to grab, select which item you want to get rid of, have your soldier hold it, and then use the Pick Up command to grab the new item and drop the old one. Here, the soldier wants to pick up the Duel Pistols, but needs to choose which weapon or loot item currently within their backpack to give up.

The above soldier chose to give up the Submachine Gun. This gun was selected, so its slot was highlighted. The soldier than picked up the Duel Pistols, while at the same time dropping the Submachine Gun (which is now lying on the ground).

Once you've collected two or more weapons and they're being carried in your soldier's backpack, to ensure you'll be able to access the most powerful and useful weapons quickly, consider re-organizing your backpack inventory. Shown here, from left to right, this soldier has a Burst Assault Rifle, Semi-Automatic Sniper Rifle, Shield Potion, Submachine Gun, and Suppressed Pistol.

To move the Burst Assault Rifle to the right, first select it. When the arrows icon appears over the item, move it to the right, to the location where you want it, and then place it there. Keep repeating this process until the soldier's inventory is positioned in the slots that make the most sense.

After some re-arranging, from left to right, the order of the weapons and items is now Semi-Automatic Sniper Rifle, Submachine Gun, Burst Assault Rifle, Suppressed Pistol, and Shield Potion. As you can see, they're arranged from long-range, to mid-range, to close-range, with the powerup loot item on the extreme right.

In this case, you could easily free up one backpack slot by consuming the Shield Potion, since the soldier's Shield meter is currently at zero. Remember, anytime you choose to re-arrange your soldier's backpack, make sure he or she is hiding in a secluded or well-protected area, so no enemies can attack while your attention is focused elsewhere.

HOW WEAPONS ARE CATEGORIZED AND RATED

Some of the weapon category types in *Fortnite: Battle Royale* include:

- Assault Rifles
- Explosives (See Section 5 — Taking Advantage of Loot Items that Serve as Weapons for more information about Grenades, Remote Explosives, Stink Bombs, Impulse Grenades, and other explosive weapons that are considered loot items.)
- Machine Guns
- Pistols

- Projectile Explosive Weapons (Launchers)
- Shotguns
- SMGs (Submachine Guns)
- Sniper Rifles

Within each category of weapon, there are at least several individual types of weapons. For example, within the SMG (Submachine Gun) category, there are Compact SMGs, Drum Guns, and Suppressed Submachine Guns. In the Pistol category, you'll discover Hand Cannons, Revolvers, Duel Pistols, Suppressed Pistols, and regular handheld Pistols.

Each type of weapon can also be classified as a short-range, mid-range, long-range, or as an explosive weapon. Thus, based on your current situation, you always want to choose the most suitable weapon that's at your disposal.

The power and capabilities of each weapon is measured in a variety of ways, including: Rarity, Bullet/Ammunition Type, Damage Per Second (DPS), Damage, Fire Rate, MAG Size, and Reload Time.

RARITY

A weapon's Rarity helps to determine its overall power and capabilities. The same type of weapon can typically be found on the island with different Rarity classifications.

Weapons displayed with a grey hue and banner are considered "common." These are the weakest, but most widely available weapons.

Weapons displayed with a green hue and banner are classified as "uncommon."

Weapons displayed with a blue hue and banner are "rare."

Weapons with a purple hue and banner are "epic."

Weapons with an orange hue and banner are "legendary." These are the most powerful and difficult to find during a match.

As you're exploring the island, anytime you come across a "legendary" weapon, grab it, even if you already have the same weapon in your arsenal, but the one you have has a lesser Rarity.

BULLET/AMMUNITION TYPE

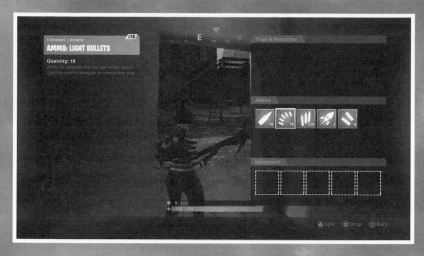

There are five different types of ammunition that work with the various guns available on the island. These include Heavy Bullets, Light Bullets, Medium Bullets, Rockets, and Shells. How much of each type of ammunition your soldier has collected is displayed on the Backpack Inventory screen.

Section 4—Collecting and Using Ammunition explains each type of ammunition, how it's used, and how it gets collected. Once you've acquired different types of guns, unless you have the right type of ammunition to go with it, that weapon will be useless.

DAMAGE PER SECOND (DPS)

Anytime you access the Backpack Inventory screen and highlight a specific type of gun you're holding, details about it are displayed in the top-right corner of the screen (on most gaming systems). DPS (which stands for Damage Per Second) is an indication of how much damage that weapon can cause per second if you press and hold down the trigger.

A weapon's DPS is calculated based on its clip (magazine) size, damage per round, and fire rate. Thus, when you see a weapon with a high DPS rating, this is a really good indication that the weapon is powerful and can cause significant damage.

Weapons with a small magazine (clip) size, that can only shoot a small number of rounds before it needs reloading, will always have a low DPS rating, because you can only shoot a few rounds per second.

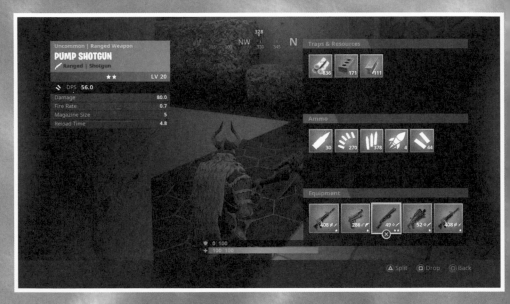

An "uncommon" Pump Shotgun, for example, has a DPS rating of 56. Its Damage rating is 80, while its Fire Rate is 0.7 round per second, and its Magazine Size is 5. Its Reload Time is 4.8 seconds.

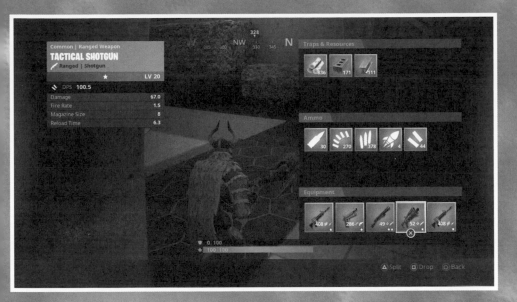

A "common" Tactical Shotgun has a DPS rating of 100.5. Its Damage rating is 67, while its Fire Rate is 1.5 rounds per second. Its Magazine Size is 8, and its Reload Time is 6.3.

DAMAGE

This is a numeric indication of how much HP damage a single round from a gun can cause per direct hit. A Pistol (one of the weaker weapons available) has a Damage rating between 23 and 25, while a direct hit from a round shot from a Rocket Launcher has a Damage rating of over 120.

FIRE RATE

This refers to how many rounds the gun can shoot per second, as long as it has enough ammunition. Some of the more powerful guns have a slow Fire Rate, which means each bullet (if it hits its target) will cause a decent level of damage, but if you miss the shot, you'll need to wait longer before taking the next shot.

Submachine Guns, for example, have a very fast Fire Rate (typically between 9 and 13 rounds per seconds), while a Bolt-Action Sniper Rifle, for example, has a Fire Rate of just 0.33. It only holds one bullet at a time before it needs to be reloaded.

MAGAZINE (MAG) SIZE

The MAG or clip size tells you how many rounds of ammunition (or bullets) a weapon can hold at once, before it needs to be reloaded. Some weapons, like Bolt-Action Sniper Rifles (with a Scope) have a very small magazine size and can hold just one shell round at a time before it needs to be reloaded. A Compact Submachine Gun, however, has a MAG size of 50, and a Light Machine Gun has a MAG size of 100.

RELOAD TIME

Once you've shot all of the ammo the selected weapon can hold at once, it'll need to be reloaded. How long it takes to reload each weapon type varies from about 1.5 seconds to 6.3 seconds.

If you're using a gun with a long reload time, you have a few options. For example, while the gun is reloading, crouch down and hide somewhere safe, since you can't fire the weapon while its reloading.

Alternatively, quickly switch to a different gun that your soldier has within their backpack, aim the new weapon, and continue firing.

Another option is to collect and store two identical weapons in side-by-side slots within your soldier's backpack. As soon as one weapon needs to reload, quickly switch to the other, and continue firing. The amount of time it takes to switch weapons is often less than the reload time of some weapons. Shown here, the two sniper rifles were placed side-by-side within the left-most backpack slots.

Many weapons with a slower reload time tend to be more powerful than weapons with a fast reload time. Remember, you'll need to protect your soldier during the reload period.

LEARN MORE ABOUT THE LATEST WEAPONS

There are several websites you can visit to learn more about how all of the weapons in *Fortnite: Battle Royale* are categorized and rated. These websites are updated regularly and provide the current stats for each weapon based on the latest tweaks made to the game. Just make sure when you look at this information online, it refers to the most recently released version of *Fortnite: Battle Royale*.

Three of the websites worth visiting include:

- IGN.com - www.ign.com/wikis/fortnite/Weapons
- Gameskinny.com - www.gameskinny.com/9mt22/complete-fortnite-battle-royale-weapons-stats-list
- RankedBoost.com - https://rankedboost.com/fortnite/best-weapons-tier-list

STRATEGIES FOR IMPROVING YOUR AIM WITH GUNS

Only when you're using a weapon properly will it cause the most possible damage per shot. For example, a headshot made with a Pistol at close range will pack a wallop, but if you're far away from your target and shoot with a Pistol, it'll cause much less damage because a Pistol is a close-range weapon.

In general, the farther you get from your enemy, the less damage a weapon will cause per direct hit. Regardless of the gun type, a headshot always causes more damage than a body shot.

Accuracy of a weapon improves when your soldier is standing still (as opposed to walking or running).

When your soldier crouches down and aims a weapon, its accuracy improves even more. A weapon's accuracy also improves, often dramatically, when you press the Aim button and first aim your weapon at your target before pulling the trigger.

As you're aiming a weapon, notice that the size of the crosshair changes. The bullets or ammo you shoot will likely land somewhere within that crosshair. When the crosshair is larger, this means there's a wider area in which your bullets will land. Based on what you're doing (crouching, standing still, walking, running, or jumping, for example), the size of the crosshair will automatically change. Ideally, you want to see the smallest crosshair possible to ensure the greatest accuracy when you pull the trigger. This soldier is shooting against a solid-colored hill to make it easier to see the weapon's targeting crosshair.

This soldier is jumping and shooting at the same time. If you look closely, the crosshair is very large, which means the area where the bullet(s) will land is expanded. (A large crosshair translates to less-accurate aim.)

Here, the soldier is crouching down (not moving) and shooting the same weapon, from the same distance, at the mountain. Notice the crosshair is much smaller.

To improve your aim, don't just hold down the trigger to keep firing the same weapon. The longer you hold down the trigger, the worse the weapon's accuracy will become. Instead, shoot in short bursts.

While it's always better to achieve a headshot, which will cause maximum damage on an enemy, it's often more practical to aim for the enemy's body (which is a larger area to target). This will improve your chances of a hit, especially when you're farther away from the target.

Most top-ranked *Fortnite: Battle Royale* players agree that one of the most versatile weapons is any type of Shotgun. These can be used at almost any distance from your target, yet still cause damage. For long-range shots, however, your best bet is to use a rifle with a scope.

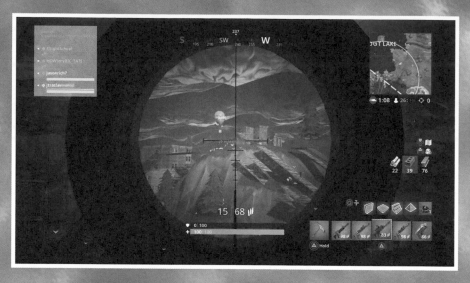

A rifle with a thermal scope allows you to see enemies when they're hiding behind objects or see their location when they're hiding within a fortress.

Use a thermal scope (or regular scope) like binoculars to spy on enemies from far away. If the enemy pops his or her head out in the open, use this weapon to shoot. Otherwise, if they're hiding within a fort, consider using a projectile explosive weapon, such as a Grenade Launcher, Rocket Launcher, or Guided Missile Launcher to destroy the fort, and at the same time, injure or defeat whomever is hiding inside.

Anytime you're using a Sniper Rifle to pick off a target that's very far away (100 yards or more), you'll need to consider a phenomenon known as "bullet drop." As the bullet is traveling over a long distance, it will drop down a bit as it follows its trajectory. Thus, you'll want to aim a bit higher than where your intended target actually is.

Regardless of which weapon you're holding, when you aim it, it'll be held on your soldier's right side or right shoulder. Knowing this, as you're shooting, try to keep the left side of your soldier's body protected by partially hiding behind an object or wall, for example. Here, most of the soldier's body is protected by the metal wall.

Here, the soldier is on the opposite end of the same wall. To shoot, almost all her body (the left side) is now fully exposed.

Remember, it's always better to be higher up than your enemy, so you're shooting at them in a downward direction.

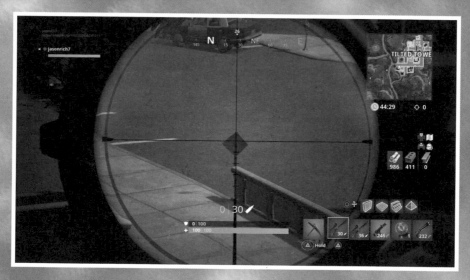

The best way to improve your targeting skills using a sniper rifle (or any weapon for that matter) is to practice. Start by practicing on targets that are not moving. When in Playground mode or when you're alone in an area of the island, use a street sign or small object as your practice target. Keep moving farther away, while keeping the target in your line of sight, and figure out what you need to adjust to continue hitting that target.

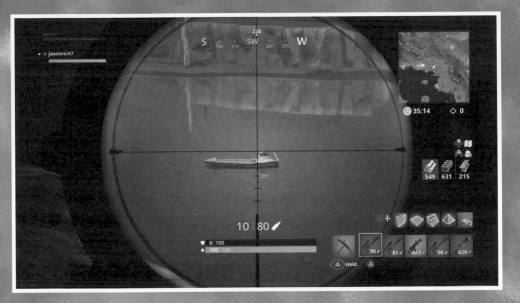

As you're working on your aiming skills, find non-moving objects on the island that you know your enemies will approach, such as a chest. Get in position and aim right next to the object. Now just wait for an enemy soldier to approach, and then fire the sniper rifle when the target is perfectly positioned within your sights.

Remember, how much damage a weapon causes depends on several factors, including the weapon type, your distance from the enemy, the accuracy of your aim, the weapon's rarity, and its DPS rating.

Even when it comes to shooting long-distance weapons (such as a sniper rifle with a scope, Rocket Launcher, Grenade Launcher, or Guided Missile Launcher), the farther away you are from your target, the less damage a direct hit will cause, and the less accurate your aim will be.

HOW TO AIM A PROJECTILE EXPLOSIVE WEAPON

Three of the more destructive weapons at your disposal are projectile explosive weapons. These include the Rocket Launcher, Grenade Launcher, and Guided Missile Launcher. All three can be used to destroy buildings, fortresses, and structures, and at the same time injure or defeat any enemies within them.

Rocket Launchers, Grenade Launchers, and Guided Missile Launchers each come in three different Rarities—"Rare" (Blue), "Epic" (Purple), and "Legendary" (Orange). The Legendary version always has the highest Damage rating.

These weapons are designed for long-range combat. If you try shooting an enemy head-on at close range with one of these weapons, it'll do damage, but it likely won't be lethal damage. Another drawback to using these weapons simply to shoot at enemies at mid- to long-range is that an enemy will see the rockets, grenades, or missiles coming at them and can either quickly build up walls as shielding or leap out of the way (especially if they have a Bouncer Pad or Launch Pad already set up in their fortress or where they're hiding).

When shooting a Rocket Launcher from a distance, if the walls of a fortress are between you and your enemy, launch the rocket and then quickly follow up by shooting at the wall. If you can weaken or destroy the wall, the rocket from the Rocket Launcher will potentially do more damage to your enemy.

You'll typically cause more damage and havoc if you're able to shoot a projectile explosive weapon directly into an enemy base (through an open door or window, or from above if there's no roof), as opposed to shooting directly into a wall of an enemy fortress or structure.

You can also use the rocket or guided missile to break through an enemy barrier or fortress wall, and then quickly follow up by shooting a gun in order to finish off the enemies inside.

When shooting a Grenade Launcher, keep in mind that like the handheld Grenades you toss, these will bounce off a solid object, so if you're too close, you could wind up getting caught in the explosion. You're much better off shooting these through an open door, window, or into the top of a structure that has no roof. Here, the soldier is standing a good distance away from a small metal structure that an enemy may be hiding behind. When the soldier aims the Grenade Launcher directly at the wall, the Grenade bounces of the wall, back toward the soldier.

As you can see, the resulting explosion is very close to the soldier who fired the Grenade Launcher, and the actual target is undamaged.

A much better strategy using the Grenade Launcher would be to get up higher than the enemy fortress (in this case by climbing up onto a small nearby hill) and then shooting downward, directly into the enemy's structure (from above).

Here's another example of how a Grenade Launcher can be used to "drop" Grenades into an enemy fortress from above (assuming there's no roof on the structure). Using this approach, the Grenade(s) will land inside the fortress and cause the most damage to the structure itself and whoever is inside.

Most gamers forget to build a roof when constructing their forts, so if you're shooting from above, you can aim a Grenade to land directly inside a structure. However, if you're shooting from eye level or below a fortress that has no roof, you can still choose the trajectory of the Grenade when launching it, but this requires a bit more skill. You could wind up wasting a bunch of Rockets' ammo trying to land one inside the targeted fortress.

If you're not trying to destroy a structure at the same time you're trying to take out enemies, consider using a sniper rifle with a scope for distance shooting with extreme accuracy potential. It'll take a lot of practice to get really good at shooting with a sniper rifle. Start by practicing on non-moving targets (which are easier to hit), and then work on being able to shoot accurately at moving targets.

For noobs and gamers looking to shoot with a sniper rifle, try to find and use a Semi-Automatic Sniper Rifle (shown on the left) or a Scoped Assault Rifle (shown on the right). These have a MAG size of between 10 and 20, which means you can shoot at a target up to twenty times before needing to reload.

A Bolt-Action Sniper Rifle, however, has a MAG size of just 1. If you miss your target, you'll need to wait up to three seconds to reload and shoot again (during which time your target will likely move and take cover). This is a harder weapon to shoot with because of the small MAG size and slow reload time.

ADJUST THE GAME'S SETTINGS BEFORE A MATCH TO IMPROVE YOUR AIM

From the Game menu within Settings, there are a handful of adjustable options that can help to improve your aim. Some of these options have to do with the sensitivity of the wireless controller or mouse you're using.

To access the Game menu, from the Lobby, select the main menu option, and then select the gear-shaped Settings menu. Along the top of the screen will be a series of icons representing Settings submenus. Select and highlight the Game menu.

Anytime you're adjusting an option that offers a slider, as opposed to an on/off switch, make small and subtle changes. For example, if the default setting is 0.5, don't change it to 1.0 all at once. Boost it up to 0.6 or 0.7, play a few matches, see if you like the change, and then decide whether to increase or decrease the setting based on how your controller or mouse responds. (Shown here on a PS4.)

Found under the Input heading of the Game menu on most gaming systems, the following are some of the relevant options you may want to adjust to determine how sensitive your gaming controls are, particularly when you're aiming a weapon:

Controller (Mouse) Sensitivity X—Using a slider, this option allows you to adjust the sensitivity of your wireless controller or mouse for the X axis (horizontal movement). The default setting is 0.5, but many gamers prefer this control to be more sensitive and adjust it to between 0.7 and 0.9. By doing this, you'll be able to move your soldier faster and with less effort.

Controller (Mouse) Sensitivity Y—Using a slider, this option allows you to adjust the sensitivity of your wireless controller or mouse for the Y axis (vertical movement). The default setting is 0.5, but many gamers prefer this control to be more sensitive and adjust it to between 0.7 and 0.9. By doing this, you'll be able to move your soldier faster and with less effort.

Whatever you adjust the Control (Mouse) Sensitivity X setting to should be the same as what you set the Control (Mouse) Sensitivity Y setting to, but this too is a matter of personal preference.

Controller (Mouse) Targeting Sensitivity—After pressing the Aim button to target a weapon, this option controls how sensitive the targeting controls are to your movements. The default option is 0.65, but some gamers prefer to make this option more sensitive and boost it to between 0.7 and 0.9. This is a matter of personal preference.

Controller (Mouse) Scope Sensitivity—Anytime you're using a rifle with a scope and you press the Aim button, a zoomed-in scope view is displayed, allowing you to much more precisely target your enemy. The scope targeting will be more sensitive if you boost this slider from its 0.65 default setting to between 0.7 and 0.9. Again, you'll want to experiment to determine a setting that works with your personal gaming style and equipment.

Motion Sensitivity Not Targeting—Use this option to adjust the sensitivity of the controls used to move your soldier around while he or she is not targeting a weapon. In other words, when the soldier is walking, running, jumping, or tiptoeing around the island. The more you boost this slider to the right, the more sensitive the controls will be. This option is not available on all gaming systems.

Motion Sensitivity Targeting—This option controls the sensitivity of your soldier's motion controls once the Aim button has been pressed and they're targeting a weapon (with the exception of a scoped Rifle). When you boost this slider, which is not available on all gaming systems, the target icon will be more sensitive and move with even the slightest touch. With practice, this option can help you improve your aim. Be careful not to make this function too sensitive or aiming accurately will become even more challenging.

Motion Sensitivity Scoped—This feature, which is not available on all gaming systems, works just like the Motion Sensitivity Targeting option, but is only active when you're using a Rifle with a scope and you zoom in and use the scope view to target your enemies.

Motion Sensitivity Harvesting Tool—Also not available on all gaming system, this option allows you to control how sensitive the controls will be when using your soldier's pickaxe. The more you move this slider to the right, the more sensitive the pickaxe will be to movement controls. Your soldier's pickaxe is also known as a "harvesting tool."

Toggle Targeting (On/Off)—Anytime you're using a ranged weapon and press the Aim button, aiming mode will remain until you tap the Aim button again to revert to the normal view. When this feature is turned on, you'll need to press and hold the Aim button when aiming a weapon. When aiming a weapon, your soldier moves slower if you attempt to make him/her walk, run, or tiptoe.

Aim Assist (On/Off)—Turning on this option will make it a bit easier to accurately aim your weapons. As you become really skilled at playing *Fortnite: Battle Royale*, you might want to turn off this feature to give yourself more of a challenge. However, noobs should definitely turn on this option.

After making any changes to the Game menu, be sure to use the Apply command to save your changes, and then use the Back command to return to the Lobby.

SECTION 4
COLLECTING AND USING AMMUNITION

While there are more than 100 different types of weapons that can be found, collected, and used during a match when playing *Fortnite: Battle Royale*, there are only five distinct types of ammunition you'll need to collect in order for the weapons in your arsenal to be useable.

THE FIVE TYPES OF AMMO

Light Bullets are low-caliber bullets used in handguns (including Pistols) and Submachine Guns.

Medium Bullets are mid-caliber bullets used in assault rifles and other mid-range weapons.

Heavy Bullets are high-caliber bullets used in sniper rifles.

Shells are the type of ammo used in Shotguns. Shotguns are one of the most versatile weapons offered in *Fortnite: Battle Royale*. You can use a Shotgun in a close-range firefight, as a mid-range weapon, or as a long-range weapon. However, the farther away you are from the target, the less accurate your aim will be and the less damage each hit from a shell will inflict.

Rockets are explosives that are used in long-range projectile explosive weapons, including Rocket Launchers, Grenade Launchers, and Guided Missile Launchers.

Without having the appropriate ammunition on hand, whatever weapons your soldier is carrying will be useless. If you attempt to fire a weapon that has no ammo available, a "Not Enough Ammo" and/or "Out of Ammo" message appears near the center and bottom-center of the screen. Your soldier will also shake his or her head.

WAYS TO FIND AND COLLECT AMMO

Throughout each match, there are several ways to find and collect ammo.

Ammunition can be collected from Ammo Boxes. Sometimes, Ammo Boxes can be found under staircases.

Ammo Boxes are scattered throughout the island, and often found within structures on shelves.

Ammo Boxes are also sometimes hidden behind objects, such as behind the counter in a shop or restaurant.

Unlike chests, they do not glow or make a sound. Many gamers don't open all the Ammo Boxes they come across. This is a mistake, because it's always better to stockpile ammo, even for weapons you don't yet have, as opposed to running out of ammo when you need it the most (during an intense firefight).

Random types of ammunition can sometimes be found out in the open, lying on the ground. You might discover that the ammo is alone (shown here).

Often, however, ammo is found in conjunction with a compatible weapon. In this case, you can grab just the weapon, just the ammo, or pick them both up and add the gun and ammo to your arsenal.

You can often grab a nice assortment of ammunition that a soldier drops immediately after they've been defeated and eliminated from a match.

Chests, Supply Drops, and Loot Llamas often contain random collections of ammunition.

Ammo can also be traded between partners, squad mates, or teammates during a Duos, Squads, or 50 v 50 match, for example. To do this, when you're close to your ally, access the Backpack Inventory screen and highlight the type of ammo you want to share. Press the Drop button.

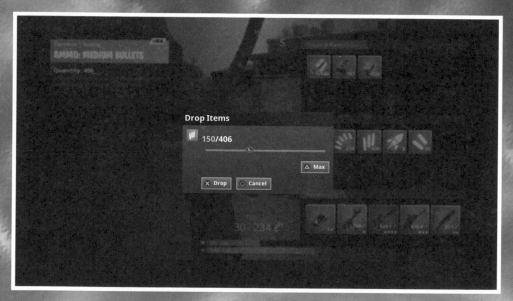

Using the displayed slider, determine how much of the selected type of ammo you're holding that you want to share. In this case, the soldier will share 150 out of 406 rounds of Medium Bullets. Press the Drop button again to drop the ammo, so your ally can pick it up.

Rockets are used within projectile explosive weapons (Rocket Launchers, Grenade Launchers, and Guided Missile Launchers). This is the hardest type of ammo to find and collect, so anytime you have the opportunity to grab some, do it! During most End Games, this type of weapon becomes almost essential, so it's a good idea to stockpile this somewhat rare type of ammo throughout the entire match.

CHOOSE YOUR ARSENAL WISELY

Based on where you are, what challenges you're currently facing, the distance you are from your target(s), and what you anticipate your needs will be, stock your backpack with the weapons and tools you think you'll need for the battles and challenges ahead.

Displayed in the bottom-right corner of the screen on most gaming systems, you can see which weapons and loot items have been placed in each backpack slot. The number you see in the bottom-right corner of each backpack slot where there's a weapon tells you how many rounds of ammo you're currently carrying.

The various types of ammunition you've collected thus far, how much of each ammo type you have on hand, and which weapons each ammo type can be used with, is displayed within the Backpack Inventory screen. While viewing the Backpack Inventory screen, select a specific ammunition type to learn more about it.

Within your backpack, you'll definitely want to include at least two or three weapons (shown in the three left-most backpack slots), as well as a handpicked selection of loot items. Having at least one explosive loot item on hand (such as Clingers), as well as at least one Health powerup loot item (in this case Bandages) will often be useful.

SECTION 5

TAKING ADVANTAGE OF LOOT ITEMS THAT SERVE AS WEAPONS

In addition to the ever-growing selection of guns available to your soldier, *Fortnite: Battle Royale* gives you access to a collection of loot items. These fall into three categories. They can be used as weapons, tools, or health and/or shield-related powerups that'll help your soldier stay alive longer. Some loot items are rare and difficult to come by. Others are much more common.

Since the focus of this strategy guide is on combat, this section's focus is only on the loot items that can be used as weapons. These items can be found and collected in the same ways as weapons or ammo. However, not all of these items require their own slot within your soldier's backpack. As you'll discover, some get stored with your soldier's resources, so to access and use them, you'll first need to enter into Building mode.

EXPLOSIVE LOOT ITEMS

The following is information and tips for using each of the weapon-oriented loot items you can find, grab, and add to your arsenal during a match. Keep in mind, it's common for Epic Games to tweak the capabilities and strength of various loot items in conjunction with a game patch (update) or the launch of a new gaming season.

LOOT ITEM	DAMAGE	MAXIMUM NUMBER YOU CAN CARRY	STORAGE LOCATION
Boogie Bombs	Once detonated (by tossing it at an enemy), this bomb causes a soldier to dance uncontrollably for five seconds. During this time, he or she is defenseless against other weapon or explosive attacks.	10	Requires one backpack inventory slot.

QUICK TIPS FOR USING BOOGIE BOMBS

Many gamers don't find a Boogie Bomb too useful, because you need to target your enemy with it, wait for them to start dancing, and then quickly follow up with another type of attack while the enemy is defenseless.

LOOT ITEM	DAMAGE	MAXIMUM NUMBER YOU CAN CARRY	STORAGE LOCATION
Bouncer Pads	If positioned correctly, these can be used to send an enemy into a bouncing loop, during which time, he or she will be defenseless against other types of attack. To use it as a weapon, you need to be creative.	Unknown	Stored with a soldier's resources, so it's accessed from Building mode, not Combat mode.

QUICK TIPS FOR USING BOUNCER PADS

This is what a Bouncer Pad looks like when it's about to be grabbed. This item gets stored with a soldier's resources and does not require a backpack slot. To place and activate this item, you'll first need to enter into Building mode.

When you position two or more of these Bouncer Pads strategically and can lure an enemy into their path, you'll be able to cause that enemy to get stuck in a repetitive bouncing loop, during which time he or she will be vulnerable to other types of attacks. An enemy can also be placed into a bouncing loop if on the opposite side of a Bouncer Pad is a solid wall.

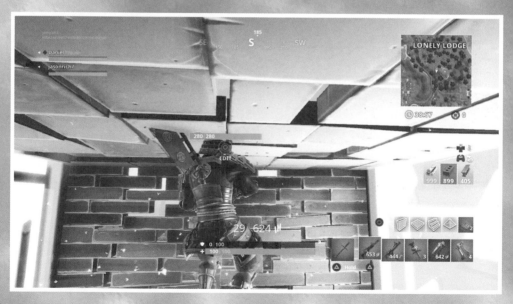

To escape if your soldier gets caught in a bounce loop, while you're bouncing, keep shooting at one of the Bouncer Pads to destroy it.

Unlike Traps or Launch Pads, for example, Bouncer Pads can be placed on a ramp and positioned at a diagonal.

LOOT ITEM	DAMAGE	MAXIMUM NUMBER YOU CAN CARRY	STORAGE LOCATION
Clingers	Up to 100 HP damage can be caused if a soldier or object is caught in the explosion. Use this to defeat enemies or blow up objects or structures.	10	Requires one backpack inventory slot.

QUICK TIPS FOR USING CLINGERS

This is what a Clinger looks like when it's about to be picked up by a soldier. When you're ready to use this item, toss one or more Clingers at an enemy soldier. It'll stick to them and can't be removed. Within a few seconds, it'll explode and cause serious damage (often defeating the enemy).

Throwing two or more Clingers at a structure (or object) will likely cause an explosion that's strong enough to damage or totally destroy that structure, whether it's a pre-made house or building, or a fortress built by an enemy. Here, one Clinger was thrown at this pickup truck.

As you can see, after the explosion, the pickup truck's HP meter went from 400/400 to 150/400.

Throwing Clingers at a moving ATK is one way to destroy the vehicle and cause mega-damage to its driver and passengers, who get caught in the explosion. Keep in mind, a Clinger takes a few seconds to detonate, so a driver or passenger of an ATK can quickly leap from the vehicle and put some distance between themselves and the explosion to lessen the impact the Clinger will have.

LOOT ITEM	DAMAGE	MAXIMUM NUMBER YOU CAN CARRY	STORAGE LOCATION
Grenades	Up to 105 HP damage can be caused if a soldier or object is caught in the explosion. Use this to defeat enemies or blow up objects or structures.	10	Requires one backpack inventory slot.

QUICK TIPS FOR USING GRENADES

This is the most common and easy to use explosive weapon.

After selecting it, the targeting crosshairs are displayed on the screen. Use your controller (keyboard/mouse) to select the target, and then toss one or more Grenades at a time. The more Grenades you toss, the bigger the explosion will be. To cause the most damage to a structure and whomever is inside, toss the Grenade through a window or open door.

Warning! Grenades will bounce off a solid object, such as a wall, and come back toward the thrower. When using them to destroy a house, building, or fortress, for example, toss Grenades through an open door or window, or if there's no roof, into the hole at the top of the fortress.

LOOT ITEM	DAMAGE	MAXIMUM NUMBER YOU CAN CARRY	STORAGE LOCATION
Impulse Grenades	When thrown at enemies, this special Grenade will catapult an enemy soldier away from the explosion's point of impact. This item does not damage structures or objects.	10	Requires one backpack inventory slot.

QUICK TIPS FOR USING IMPULSE GRENADES

If you toss an Impulse Grenade at one or more enemy soldiers who are hiding in a fort, they'll often be sent flying into the air and away from the safety of their fortress. One Impulse Grenade can impact multiple targets caught in the impact zone of this weapon.

LOOT ITEM	DAMAGE	MAXIMUM NUMBER YOU CAN CARRY	STORAGE LOCATION
Remote Explosives	Damage to enemy soldiers varies, based on how close a target is to the explosion. If placed on a structure or object, it will blow it up. Use multiple Remote Explosives together to create a bigger bang.	10	Requires one backpack inventory slot.

QUICK TIPS FOR USING REMOTE EXPLOSIVES

Unlike Grenades (which detonate as soon as they hit a target), it's necessary to manually place and activate each Remote Explosive.

Remote Explosives can be attached to almost any object, such as the wall (shown here) or door of a structure, or onto an ATK. They can also be placed near a Loot Llama, for example, to bobby trap it. Once placed, a blue light begins to flash. It's now up to the soldier who placed these explosives to wait at a safe distance, and then manually detonate them at the exact moment they want. Remote Explosives are ideal for booby trapping objects or structures.

To detonate a Remote Explosive, you can either shoot at it or hold down the Detonation button on your controller (keyboard/mouse). Many gamers find that Remote Explosives are better for destroying structures or objects than causing injury to enemies. If you place two or more Remote Explosives close together, they'll cause a bigger explosion that results in greater damage.

LOOT ITEM	DAMAGE	MAXIMUM NUMBER YOU CAN CARRY	STORAGE LOCATION
Stink Bombs	Once tossed, a Stink Bomb generates a toxic cloud of yellow smoke that lasts for 9 seconds. For every half-second an enemy is caught in the smoke, they receive 5 HP damage.	4	Requires one backpack inventory slot.

QUICK TIPS FOR USING STINK BOMBS

The biggest problem with Stink Bombs is that once an enemy soldier gets caught in its toxic cloud, he or she can easily move and start breathing safe air again, so it's rare that this weapon will cause the maximum damage that it's capable of. This type of weapon can cause the most damage if it's detonated inside a building, structure, or fortress.

LOOT ITEM	DAMAGE	MAXIMUM NUMBER YOU CAN CARRY	STORAGE LOCATION
Traps	A Trap can be placed on a wall, floor, or ceiling, or within a structure built by a soldier or a pre-existing building, for example. If an enemy gets caught by a Trap, they'll perish.	No limit	Stored with a soldier's resources, so it's accessed from Building mode, not Combat mode.

QUICK TIPS FOR USING TRAPS

A solider can find, collect, and carry multiple Traps with them. They get stored with a soldier's resources, and do not require a slot in their backpack.

Many gamers place one or more Traps at the base of their own forts to prevent enemies from invading.

While you can't place a Trap on a ramp tile, when building a ramp, you can insert one flat floor tile, place a Trap on that, and then continue building a ramp. If a soldier is chasing you up the ramp and not paying attention, the Trap will defeat them.

Here's what a Trap looks like once it's been activated on a ceiling. Once placed on a wall, floor, or ceiling, a Trap cannot be removed, unless it's shot at and destroyed. The trick is to place a Trap somewhere an enemy won't see it, so they detonate it unintentionally and immediately perish.

SECTION 6

FORTNITE: BATTLE ROYALE RESOURCES

On YouTube (www.youtube.com), Twitch.TV (www.twitch.tv/directory/game/Fortnite), or Facebook Watch (www.facebook.com/watch), in the Search field, enter the search phrase "*Fortnite: Battle Royale*" to discover many game-related channels, live streams, and prerecorded videos that'll help you become a better player.

Also, be sure to check out these online resources related to *Fortnite: Battle Royale*:

WEBSITE OR YOUTUBE CHANNEL NAME	DESCRIPTION	URL
Best *Fortnite* Settings	Discover the custom game settings used by some of the world's top-rated *Fortnite: Battle Royale* players.	www.bestfortnitesettings.com
Fandom's *Fortnite* Wiki	Discover the latest news and strategies related to *Fortnite: Battle Royale*.	http://fortnite.wikia.com/wiki/Fortnite_Wiki
Fantastical Gamer	A popular YouTuber who publishes *Fortnite* tutorial videos.	www.youtube.com/user/FantasticalGamer
FBR Insider	The *Fortnite: Battle Royale Insider* website offers game-related news, tips, and strategy videos.	www.fortniteinsider.com
Fortnite Config	An independent website that lists the custom game settings for dozens of top-rated *Fortnite: Battle Royale players*.	https://fortniteconfig.com

(continued on next page)

Fortnite Gamepedia Wiki	Read up-to-date descriptions of every weapon, loot item, and ammo type available within *Fortnite: Battle Royale*. This Wiki also maintains a comprehensive database of soldier outfits and related items released by Epic Games.	https://fortnite.gamepedia.com/Fortnite_Wiki
Fortnite Intel	An independent source of news related to *Fortnite: Battle Royale*.	www.fortniteintel.com
Fortnite Scout	Check your personal player stats, and analyze your performance using a bunch of colorful graphs and charts. Also check out the stats of other *Fortnite: Battle Royale* players.	www.fortnitescout.com
Fortnite Stats & Leaderboard	This is an independent website that allows you to view your own *Fortnite*-related stats or discover the stats from the best players in the world.	https://fortnitestats.com
Game Informer Magazine's *Fortnite* Coverage	Discover articles, reviews, and news about *Fortnite: Battle Royale* published by *Game Informer* magazine.	www.gameinformer.com/search/searchresults.aspx?q=Fortnite
Game Skinny Online Guides	A collection of topic-specific strategy guides related to *Fortnite*.	www.gameskinny.com/tag/fortnite-guides/
GameSpot's *Fortnite* Coverage	Check out the news, reviews, and game coverage related to *Fortnite: Battle Royale* that's been published by GameSpot.	www.gamespot.com/fortnite
IGN Entertainment's *Fortnite* Coverage	Check out all IGN's past and current coverage of *Fortnite*.	www.ign.com/wikis/fortnite
Jason R. Rich's Website and Social Media Feeds	Share your *Fortnite: Battle Royale* game play strategies with this book's author and learn about his other books.	www.JasonRich.com www.FortniteGameBooks.com Twitter: @JasonRich7 Instagram: @JasonRich7

Microsoft's Xbox One *Fortnite* Website	Learn about and acquire *Fortnite: Battle Royale* if you're an Xbox One gamer.	www.microsoft.com/en-US/store/p/Fortnite-Battle-Royalee/BT5P2X999VH2
MonsterDface YouTube and Twitch.tv Channels	Watch video tutorials and live game streams from an expert *Fortnite* player.	www.youtube.com/user/MonsterdfaceLive www.Twitch.tv/MonsterDface
Ninja	Check out the live and recorded game streams from Ninja, one of the most highly skilled *Fortnite: Battle Royale* players in the world on Twitch.tv and YouTube.	www.twitch.tv/ninja_fortnite_hyper www.youtube.com/user/NinjasHyper
Official Epic Games YouTube Channel for *Fortnite: Battle Royale*	The official *Fortnite: Battle Royale* YouTube channel.	www.youtube.com/user/epicfortnite
ProSettings.com	An independent website that lists the custom game settings for top-ranked *Fortnite: Battle Royale* players. This website also recommends optional gaming accessories, such as keyboards, mice, graphics cards, controllers, gaming headsets, and monitors.	www.prosettings.com/game/fortnite www.prosettings.com/best-fortnite-settings
Turtle Beach Corp.	This is one of many companies that make great quality, wired or wireless (Bluetooth) gaming headsets that work with all gaming platforms.	www.turtlebeach.com

YOUR *FORTNITE: BATTLE ROYALE* ADVENTURE CONTINUES . . .

Once you understand what's possible using the many different types of weapons available to you within *Fortnite: Battle Royale*, what will allow you to achieve success and consistently be able to defeat your enemies is practice!

Whenever Epic Games offers the Playground game play mode, this provides the perfect opportunity to spend up to 55 minutes at a time visiting the island and experimenting with the different types of guns and weapons as you participate in practice battles with your online friends (or strangers). During these mock battles, if you get defeated, your soldier will respawn moments later.

If you want to learn in real time from other gamers, participate in Duos, Squads, and 50 v 50 matches, and always pay careful attention to how other gamers react in various combat situations.

Once your soldier gets eliminated from a match, instead of quickly returning to the Lobby, take advantage of Spectator mode. Watch how the rest of the match you were participating in plays out. Be sure to study how other gamers handle firefights, prepare for the End Game, and then what they do to survive in the Final Circle.

As you're perfecting your combat skills, expect that you'll be defeated often! Learn from your mistakes. Moving forward into future matches, experiment with different ways to approach various types of situations. Also, focus on continuously improving your speed and reaction time when it comes to building, selecting and switching weapons, aiming your weapons, targeting your enemies, and taking cover when you're being shot at.

Most importantly, don't forget to have fun!